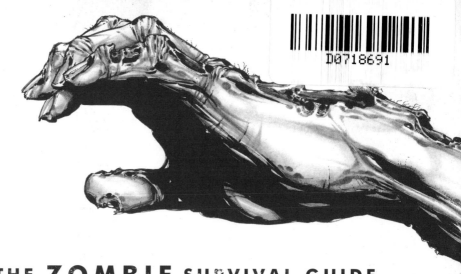

THE **ZOMBIE** SURVIVAL GUIDE

RECORDED ATTACKS

Cardiff Libraries
www.cardiff.gov.uk/libraries

Llyfrgelloedd Caerdydd
www.caerdydd.gov.uk/llyfrgelloedd

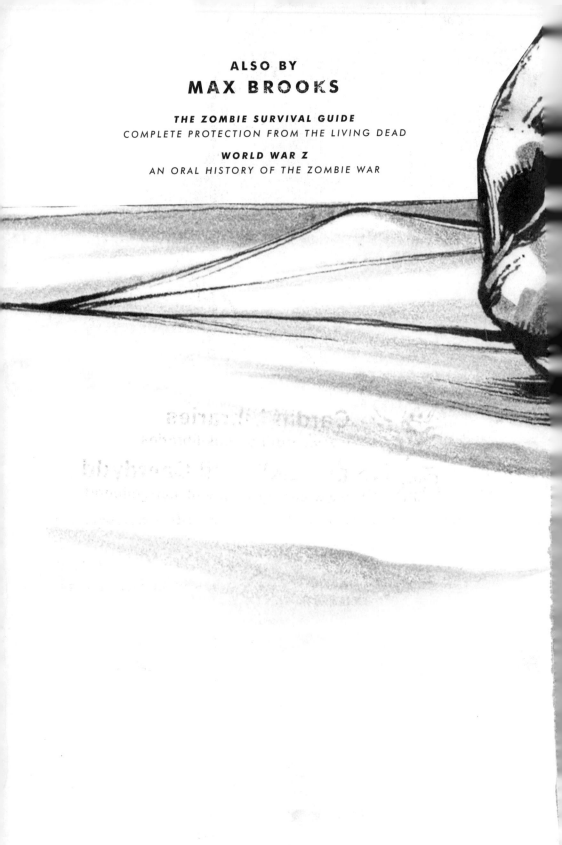

ALSO BY
MAX BROOKS

THE ZOMBIE SURVIVAL GUIDE
COMPLETE PROTECTION FROM THE LIVING DEAD

WORLD WAR Z
AN ORAL HISTORY OF THE ZOMBIE WAR

THE ZOMBIE SURVIVAL GUIDE

RECORDED ATTACKS

MAX BROOKS

Illustrated by Ibraim Roberson

Duckworth Overlook

First published in the UK in 2009 by
Duckworth Overlook
90-93 Cowcross Street, London EC1M 6BF
Tel: 020 7490 7300
Fax: 020 7490 0080
info@duckworth-publishers.co.uk
www.ducknet.co.uk

First published in the US in 2009 by Three Rivers Press, an imprint of the
Crown Publishing Group, a division of Random House, Inc., New York.
Houghton Mifflin Harcourt Publishing Company, New York

A catalogue record for this book is available
from the British Library

ISBN 978 0 7156 3815 6

Illustrations by Ibraim Roberson for Avatar Press

Printed in Great Britain

To Michelle and Henry,
my twin pillars

CONTENTS

60,000 B.C., KATANDA,
CENTRAL AFRICA

9

3000 B.C.,
HIERACONPOLIS, EGYPT

28

A.D. 121, FANUM
COCIDI, CALEDONIA

33

A.D. 1579, THE
CENTRAL PACIFIC

51

A.D. 1583, SIBERIA

58

A.D. 1611, FEUDAL JAPAN

70

A.D. 1690,
THE SOUTHERN ATLANTIC OCEAN

78

A.D. 1862, ST. LUCIA, EASTERN CARIBBEAN

88

A.D. 1893, FRENCH NORTH AFRICA

100

A.D. 1942–45, HARBIN, JAPANESE PUPPET STATE OF MANCHUKUO

115

A.D. 1960, BYELGORANSK, SOVIET UNION

123

A.D. 1992, JOSHUA TREE NATIONAL PARK

134

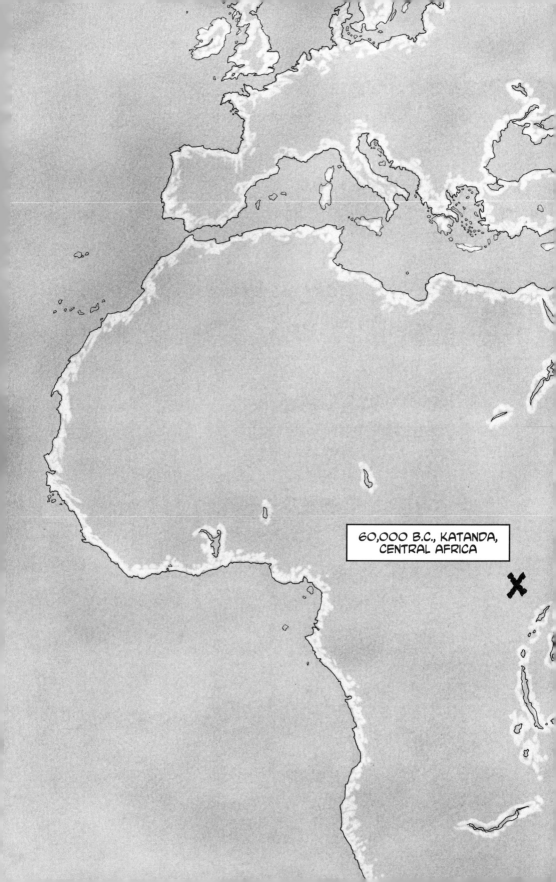

60,000 B.C., KATANDA,
CENTRAL AFRICA

RECENT ARCHAEOLOGICAL EXPEDITIONS DISCOVERED A CAVE ON THE BANKS OF THE UPPER SEMLIKI RIVER, . . .

. . . WHICH CONTAIN THIRTEEN HOMO SAPIEN SKULLS.

ALL HAVE RECEIVED FATAL TRAUMA TO THE BRAIN.

ABOVE THEM WAS DISCOVERED A PAINTING THAT MANY BELIEVE TO BE A WARNING . . .

. . . OF WHAT MAY BE HUMANITY'S FIRST (RECORDED) ENCOUNTER WITH THE LIVING DEAD.

ACADEMICS CONTINUE TO DEBATE THE EXACT MESSAGE CONVEYED IN THE CAVE PAINTING.

ONE SCHOOL OF THOUGHT CONTENDS THAT IT IS A WARNING OF THE UNDEAD'S CARNIVOROUS NATURE, . . .

. . . WHILE ANOTHER . . .

. . . BELIEVES IT TO REVEAL THE INFECTION TRANSMITTED THROUGH A ZOMBIE'S BITE . . .

. . . AND ITS EFFECT ON LIVING HUMANS.

3000 B.C.,
HIERACONPOLIS, EGYPT

A BRITISH DIG IN 1892 . . .

. . . UNEARTHED AN UNMARKED TOMB . . .

. . . CONTAINING AN OPEN SARCOPHAGUS AND A SINGLE, PARTIALLY DECOMPOSED BODY.

THOUSANDS OF SCRATCH MARKS ADORNED THE WALLS OF THE TOMB . . .

. . . AS IF THE CORPSE HAD TRIED TO CLAW ITS WAY OUT.

FORENSIC EXPERTS HAVE DETERMINED THESE MARKS TO HAVE BEEN MADE OVER THE COURSE OF SEVERAL YEARS . . .

... AND THEY EXACTLY MATCH THE WORN STATE OF THE CORPSE'S HANDS.

THE BODY ALSO DISPLAYED SEVERAL BITE MARKS ON THE RIGHT RADIUS.

BITE MARKS THAT PERFECTLY MATCH THE IMPRINT OF HUMAN TEETH.

A LATER, TWENTIETH-CENTURY AUTOPSY CONFIRMED . . .

. . . THE BRAIN'S LACK OF A FRONTAL LOBE, A PATTERN CONSISTENT WITH SOLANUM, THE VIRUS RESPONSIBLE FOR THE LIVING DEAD.

FURTHER ANALYSIS UNCOVERED MINUTE EXAMPLES OF THE VIRUS ITSELF, THE OLDEST KNOWN SAMPLES ON RECORD.

A.D. 121, FANUM
COCIDI, CALEDONIA

THE NATURE OF THE OUTBREAK WAS CLEARLY LOST ON THE LOCAL CHIEFTAIN, . . .

. . . WHO BELIEVED THE LIVING DEAD TO SIMPLY BE INSANE . . .

. . . AND UTTERLY HARMLESS.

TUBERO BARELY ESCAPED
WITH HIS LIFE TO THE CLOSEST
ROMAN OUTPOST . . .

. . . AND REPORTED HIS FINDINGS
TO ITS COMMANDER, MARCUS
LUCIUS TERENTIUS, . . .

. . . THAT A SWARM OF
OVER 9,000 "CREATURES"
WERE ON THE MOVE, . . .

. . . FOLLOWING THE
FLEEING REFUGEES
SOUTH . . .

. . . TOWARD
ROMAN TERRITORY.

TERENTIUS GATHERED A FORCE OF CIVILIAN LABORERS, . . .

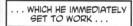

. . . WHICH HE IMMEDIATELY SET TO WORK . . .

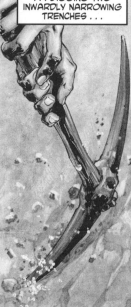

. . . DIGGING TWO INWARDLY NARROWING TRENCHES . . .

. . . AND REINFORCED PALISADES.

THE BOTTOM OF EACH TRENCH WAS LINED WITH STAKES AND FILLED WITH BITUMEN LIQUIDUM (CRUDE OIL).

... UNLUCKY ENOUGH TO BE BITTEN.

THE HARSH LESSONS LEARNED THAT DAY WERE INCORPORATED INTO THE ROMAN STANDARD COMBAT DOCTRINE.

THIS BECAME KNOWN, SIMPLY, AS "ARMY ORDER THIRTY-EIGHT," . . .

. . . WHICH WAS READ TO EVERY LEGION . . .

. . . IN EVERY CORNER OF THE ROMAN EMPIRE.

SOME SAY IT PROMPTED EMPEROR HADRIAN TO CONSTRUCT A MASSIVE WALL ACROSS THE ENTIRE WIDTH OF NORTHERN BRITAIN . . .

. . . TO GUARD AGAINST AN ENEMY . . .

. . . ALL FEARED WOULD RISE AGAIN.

A.D. 1579, THE
CENTRAL PACIFIC

... AND LANDED IN SEARCH OF PROVISIONS.

THE NATIVES WARNED HIM NOT TO VISIT A NEARBY CAY, ...

... WHERE THE "GODS OF THE DEAD" WOULD TAKE THE TRIBE'S DECEASED* AND TERMINALLY ILL TO LIVE WITH THEM FOR ALL ETERNITY.

*MOST SCHOLARS AGREE THAT DRAKE MUST HAVE MISUNDERSTOOD THE CONCEPT OF "DECEASED," BECAUSE THE SOLANUM VIRUS HAS NO REANIMATE POWERS UPON DEAD FLESH.

DRAKE WAS FASCINATED BY THEIR STORY, . . .

. . . AND SOMEHOW "CONVINCED THE ISLAND CHIEF" . . .

. . . TO GIVE HIM A DEMONSTRATION OF THE ISLAND'S SUPPOSED SECRET OF IMMORTALITY.

PERHAPS DRAKE BELIEVED HE HAD STUMBLED UPON A PACIFIC SOURCE OF THE LEGENDARY FOUNTAIN OF YOUTH.

IF SO, . . .

DRAKE NEVER SPOKE OF THIS INCIDENT DURING HIS LIFE.

THE FACTS WERE DISCLOSED IN A SECRET JOURNAL HE KEPT HIDDEN UNTIL HIS DEATH.

ALONG WITH EXACT COORDINATES OF THE "ISLE OF THE DAMNED."

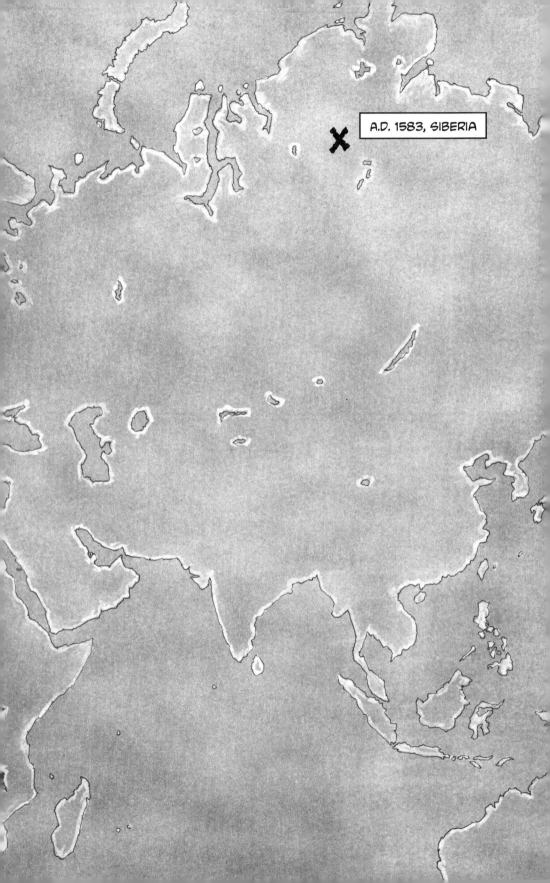

A.D. 1583, SIBERIA

DURING THE RUSSIAN EXPANSION FROM EUROPE INTO ASIA, A SCOUTING PARTY FOR THE INFAMOUS COSSACK YERMAK, BECAME SEPARATED FROM THE MAIN FORCE . . .

. . . AND WOULD HAVE UNDOUBTEDLY PERISHED FROM COLD AND STARVATION . . .

. . . HAD THEY NOT BEEN RESCUED BY A VILLAGE OF NATIVE SIBERIANS.

AFTER DEVOURING THE VILLAGE'S ENTIRE FOOD SUPPLY, THE COSSACKS QUICKLY TURNED TO THE VILLAGERS THEMSELVES.

THE COSSACKS EXHAUSTED THIS NEW SOURCE OF FOOD WITHIN DAYS, AND SUBSEQUENTLY TURNED TO THE VILLAGE'S BURIAL GROUND, . . .

. . . WHERE THEY HOPED THAT THE FREEZING TEMPERATURES . . .

. . . HAD PRESERVED SOME OF THE BODIES.

THE ONLY "FRESH" CORPSE THEY FOUND WAS A WOMAN IN HER MID-TWENTIES.

HER HANDS . . .

. . . AND FEET WERE BOUND, . . .

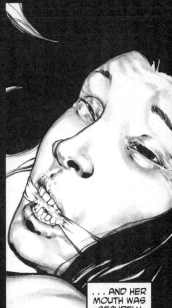

. . . AND HER MOUTH WAS SECURELY GAGGED.

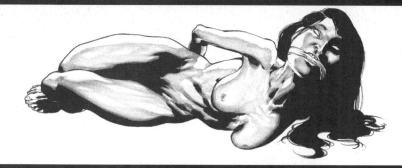

THE COSSACKS, NOT UNDERSTANDING THE NATURE OF WHAT THEY HAD JUST THAWED, . . .

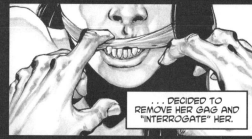

. . . DECIDED TO REMOVE HER GAG AND "INTERROGATE" HER.

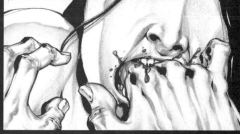

THEY RESPONDED IN TYPICAL COSSACK FASHION . . .

. . . BY CHOPPING UP THE UNDEAD WOMAN'S BODY, . . .

. . . ROASTING IT, . . .

. . . AND EATING IT ANYWAY.

ONLY TWO COSSACKS ABSTAINED FROM THE FEAST:

THE WOUNDED MAN, WHO BECAME FAR TOO ILL TO EAT, . . .

. . . AND ANOTHER, WHO BELIEVED THE MEAT OF THE UNDEAD WOMAN WAS CURSED.

THIS LONE SURVIVOR REPORTED THAT ONLY ONE OF HIS COMRADES, THE ONE BITTEN BY THE UNDEAD WOMAN, REANIMATED NOT LONG AFTER HIS DEATH . . .

. . . AND ATTEMPTED TO PURSUE HIM . . .

. . . BEFORE SUCCUMBING TO THE ELEMENTS . . .

. . . AND FREEZING SOLID.

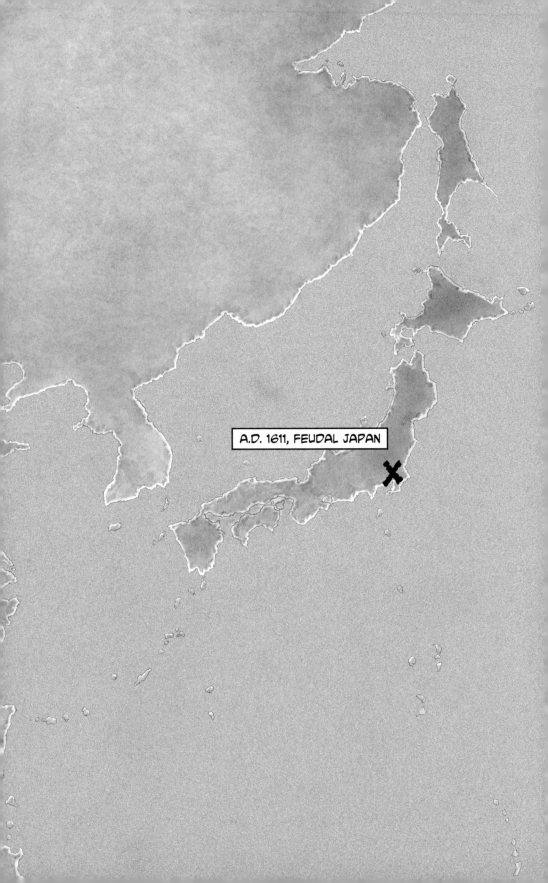

ENRIQUE DESILVA, A PORTUGUESE MERCHANT ON A TRADE MISSION TO THE ISLANDS, ...

... WROTE IN A LETTER TO HIS BROTHER:

"FATHER MENDOZA, ...

"... HAVING REACQUAINTED HIMSELF WITH CASTILIAN WINE, ..."

"... SPOKE OF A RECENT CONVERT TO OUR FAITH, ..."

"... WHO WAS ONCE PART OF A SECRET SOCIETY ..."

"... CALLING THEMSELVES THE 'BROTHERHOOD OF LIFE.'"*

*SUBSEQUENT RESEARCH HAS UNCOVERED THAT THE ORGANIZATION'S TRUE NAME WAS THE TATENOKAI, OR "SHIELD SOCIETY."

"HE CLAIMS THIS SECRET SOCIETY EXISTS FOR THE SOLE PURPOSE OF EXTERMINATING CURSED SOULS ..."

"... THAT HAVE RISEN FROM THEIR GRAVES ..."

"... TO PREY UPON THE FLESH OF THE LIVING."

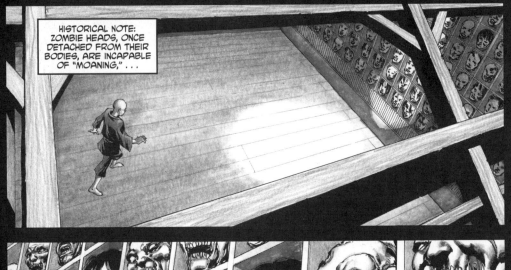

HISTORICAL NOTE: ZOMBIE HEADS, ONCE DETACHED FROM THEIR BODIES, ARE INCAPABLE OF "MOANING," . . .

. . . WHICH EITHER EXPOSES THE HYPERBOLE OF FATHER MENDOZA . . .

. . . OR EXPLAINS A DEEP, PSYCHOLOGICAL TORTURE, . . .

. . . IN WHICH THE MOANS OF HEADS WERE SIMPLY IMAGINED . . .

. . . THROUGH SHEER TERROR.

THIS MIGHT HAVE BEEN THE SHIELD SOCIETY'S WAY OF TESTING THEIR RECRUITS' METTLE WHEN CONFRONTING THE LIVING DEAD.

EITHER THE YOUNG WARRIORS SURRENDERED TO THEIR FEAR, . . .

. . . OR . . .

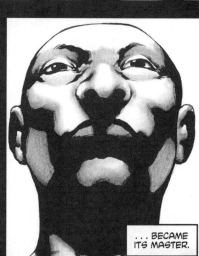

. . . BECAME ITS MASTER.

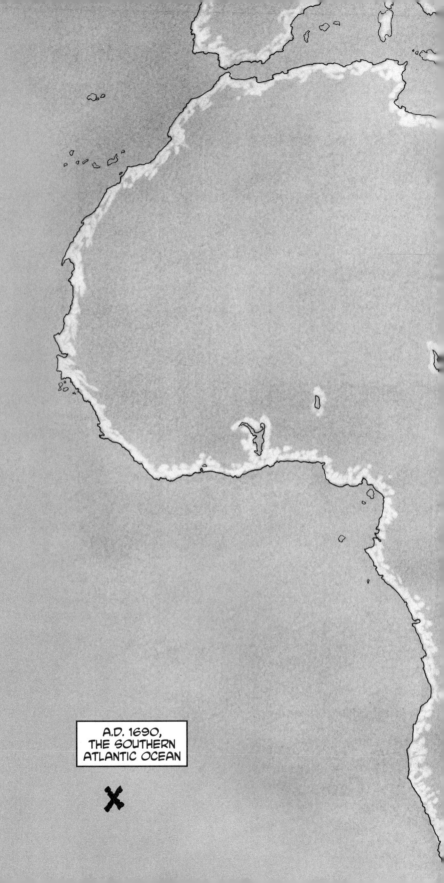

A.D. 1690,
THE SOUTHERN
ATLANTIC OCEAN

THE PORTUGUESE MERCHANTMAN *MARIALVA*...

...DEPARTED BISSAU, WEST AFRICA, FOR RECIFE, ON THE COAST OF BRAZIL,...

...WITH A CARGO...

...OF AFRICAN SLAVES.

SHE NEVER REACHED HER DESTINATION.

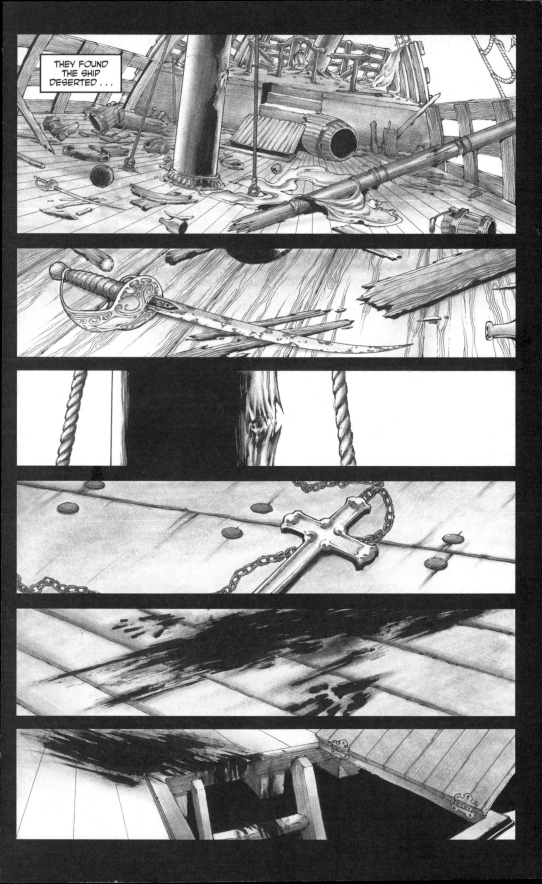

. . . AND A HOLD
FULL OF UNDEAD.

THE DANES, BELIEVING THE *MARIALVA* TO BE CURSED . . .

. . . ROWED HASTILY BACK TO THEIR OWN SHIP . . .

. . . AND SANK THE INFESTED VESSEL WITH CANNON FIRE.

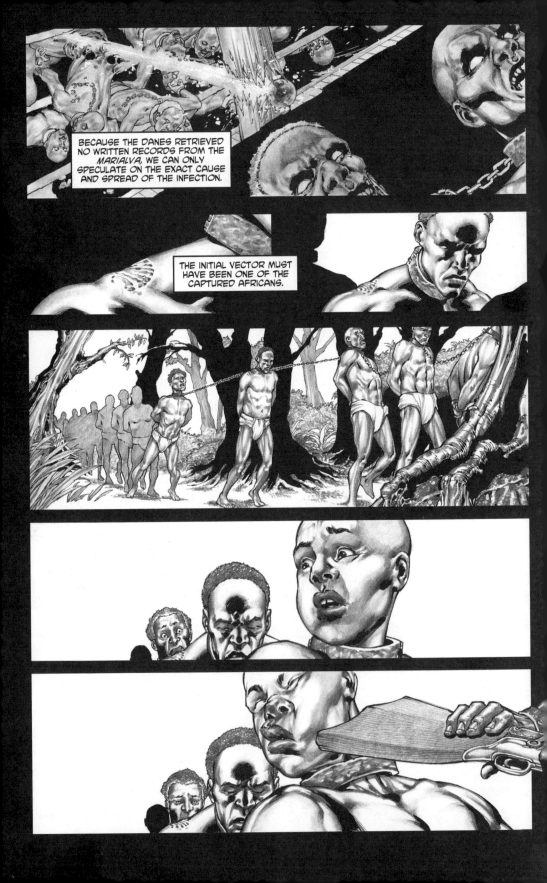

BECAUSE THE DANES RETRIEVED NO WRITTEN RECORDS FROM THE *MARIALVA*, WE CAN ONLY SPECULATE ON THE EXACT CAUSE AND SPREAD OF THE INFECTION.

THE INITIAL VECTOR MUST HAVE BEEN ONE OF THE CAPTURED AFRICANS.

PERHAPS THE ORIGINAL SLAVE TRADERS DID NOT KNOW OF THE UNDEAD PLAGUE THEY WERE UNLEASHING UPON THEIR EUROPEAN PARTNERS, . . .

. . . OR PERHAPS THEY DID.

MANY HAVE SPECULATED THAT THE INFECTION NOT ONLY RIPPED THROUGH THE PORTUGUESE CREW, . . .

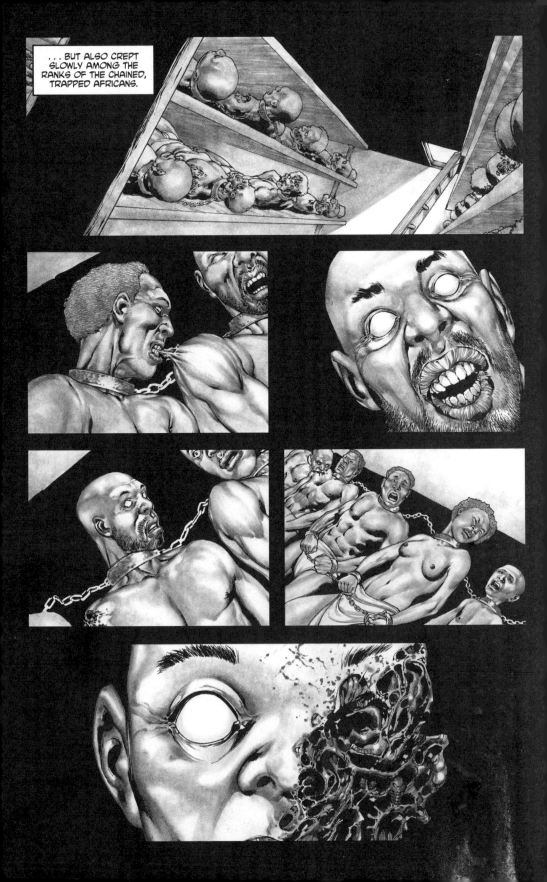

... BUT ALSO CREPT SLOWLY AMONG THE RANKS OF THE CHAINED, TRAPPED AFRICANS.

THE TRUE COURSE OF
EVENTS ABOARD THE
PORTUGUESE SLAVE SHIP
REMAINS A MYSTERY, . . .

. . . AS DOES THE
ULTIMATE FATE
OF HER CARGO.

A.D. 1862, ST. LUCIA,
EASTERN CARIBBEAN

THE FIRST REANIMATED INDIVIDUALS WERE RESTRAINED . . .

. . . AND INCARCERATED, . . .

. . . WHILE THE BITTEN WHITES WERE SENT HOME, WITHOUT TREATMENT . . .

. . . OR WARNING OF WHAT LAY AHEAD.

THE REMAINING WHITES FLED TO THE OUTLYING SUGAR PLANTATIONS, . . .

. . . CARRYING THE INFECTION TO EVERY CORNER OF THE ISLAND.

WITHIN TEN DAYS, ALMOST THE ENTIRE WHITE POPULATION OF ST. LUCIA WAS EITHER DEAD OR REANIMATED.

THE REMAINING SURVIVORS EITHER FLED BY SEA . . .

. . . OR SOUGHT REFUGE IN THE ISLAND'S TWO FORTRESSES OF VIEUX FORT AND RODNEY BAY, . . .

. . . COMPLETELY ABANDONING THEIR THOUSANDS OF BLACK SLAVES TO THE LIVING DEAD.

UNLIKE THE EUROPEAN COLONISTS, THE DESCENDANTS OF AFRICA KNEW EXACTLY WHAT THEY WERE FACING.

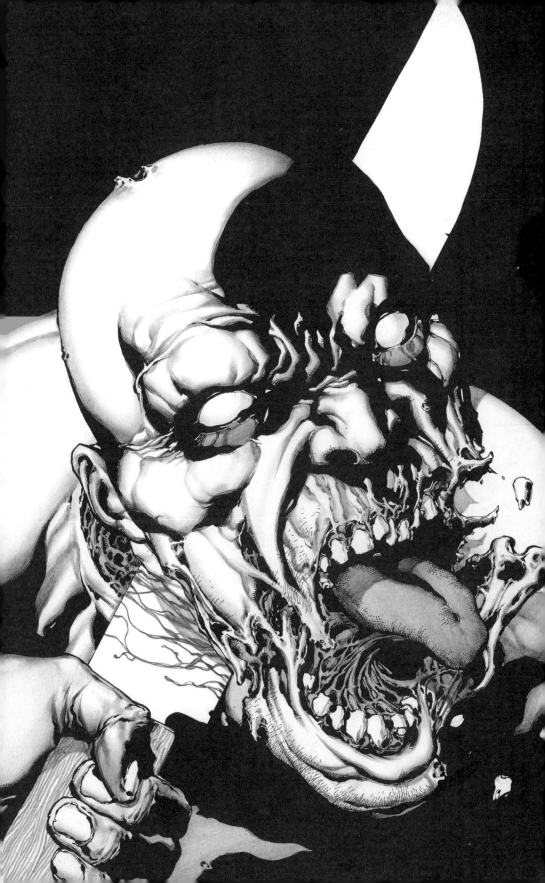

OFFICIAL RECORDS IN LONDON AND PARIS DESCRIBE THE INCIDENT AS A "SLAVE REVOLT."

ALL FORMER SLAVES WERE RECAPTURED AND PLACED BACK ON THEIR RESPECTIVE PLANTATIONS.

ALL FREE BLACKS AND MULATTOS WERE HANGED.

NO OFFICIAL ACCOUNTS EVER MENTION THE EXISTENCE OF THE LIVING DEAD.

A.D. 1893, FRENCH
NORTH AFRICA

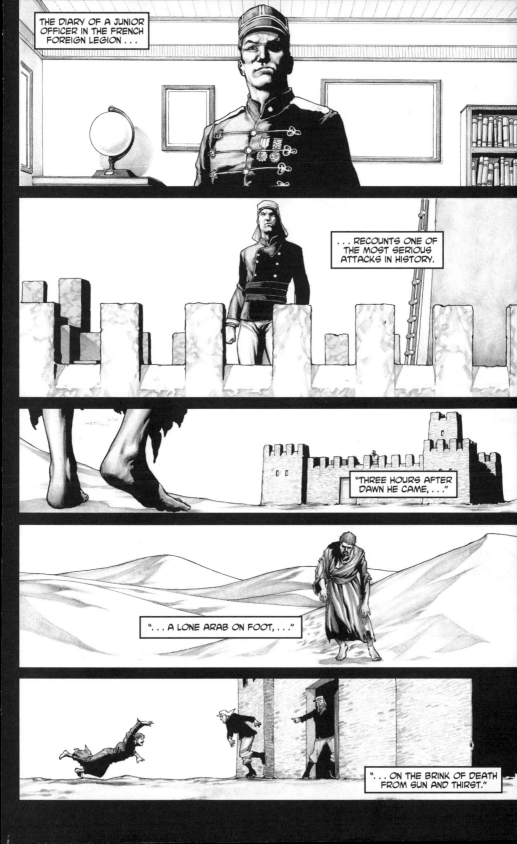

"HE RELATED A STORY OF A PLAGUE THAT TURNED ITS VICTIMS INTO CANNIBALISTIC HORRORS."

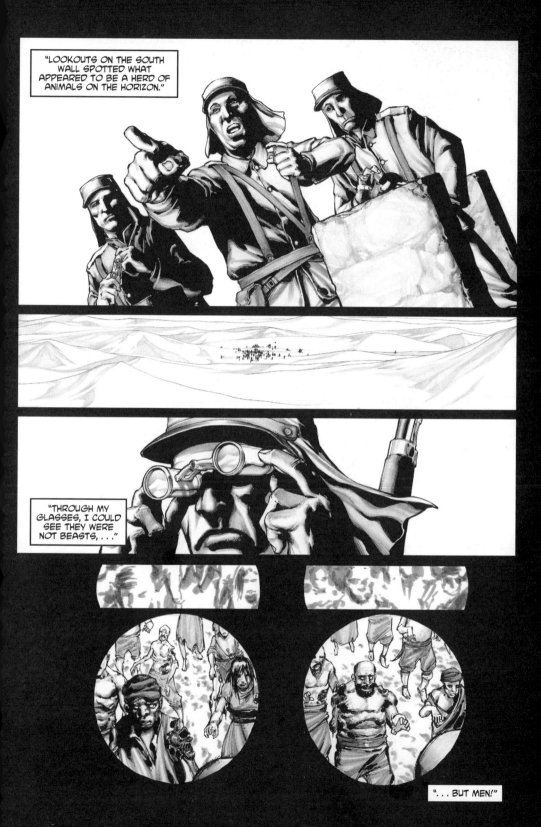

"AS THE WIND SHIFTED, . . ."

". . . IT BROUGHT TO US . . ."

". . . FIRST A WITHERING GROAN, . . ."

". . . THEN THE STENCH OF HUMAN DECAY."

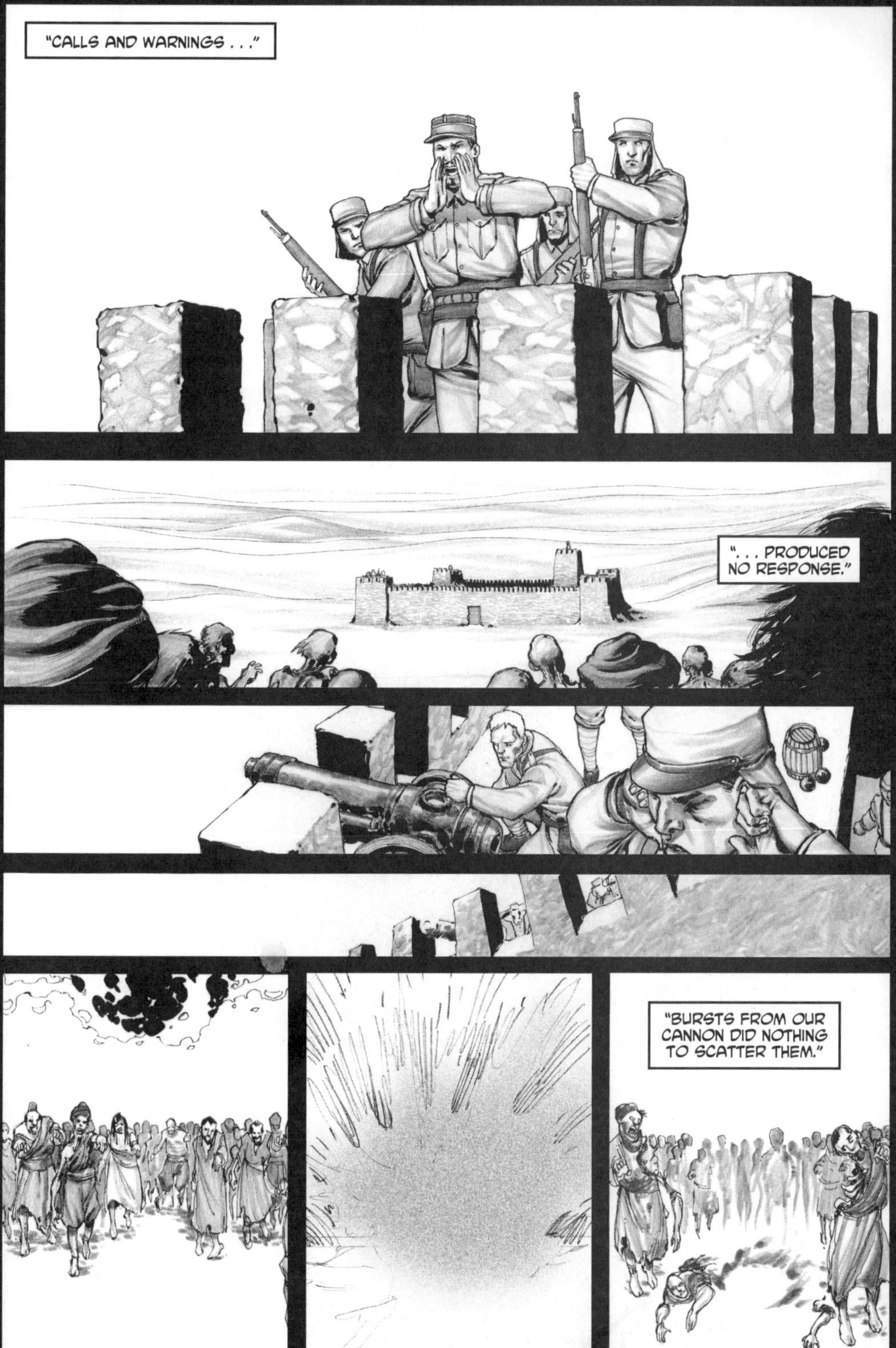

"CALLS AND WARNINGS . . ."

". . . PRODUCED NO RESPONSE."

"BURSTS FROM OUR CANNON DID NOTHING TO SCATTER THEM."

"LONG-RANGE RIFLE SHOTS SEEMED TO HAVE NO EFFECT!"

"CORPORAL STROM WAS DISPATCHED TO BIR-EL-KSAIB . . ."

". . . WHILE WE SHUT THE GATES AND PREPARED FOR AN ATTACK."

THE ATTACK TURNED INTO THE LONGEST RECORDED SIEGE IN HISTORY.

THE LEGIONNAIRES WERE UNABLE TO GRASP THE FACT THAT THEIR ATTACKERS WERE DEAD, . . .

. . . WASTING THEIR AMMUNITION ON SHOTS TO THE TORSO.

ACCIDENTAL, BUT SUCCESSFUL, HEAD SHOTS . . .

. . . WERE NOT ADOPTED BY THE LEGIONNAIRES, . . .

. . . EITHER BECAUSE OF STRICT ADHERENCE TO BATTLE DOCTRINE, OR SIMPLE BLIND PANIC.

CORPORAL STROM, THE MAN SENT FOR HELP, WAS NEVER HEARD FROM AGAIN.

WHILE HIS COMRADES . . .

. . . REMAINED TRAPPED . . .

. . . FOR THREE YEARS.

WITH THEIR AMMUNITION WASTED WITHIN THE FIRST FEW DAYS, THE LEGIONNAIRES COULD DO NOTHING BUT TRY TO SURVIVE UNTIL HELP CAME.

IT NEVER DID.

THE UNDEAD HORDE CONTINUED TO SURROUND THE FORT, . . .

. . . WHICH DROVE SOME MEN TO SUICIDE . . .

. . . AND OTHERS . . .

. . . TO ATTEMPT LEAPING OVER THE UNDEAD AND RUNNING FOR SAFETY.

THEY DIDN'T MAKE IT VERY FAR.

FINALLY, WITH THE MEN ON THE VERGE OF MUTINY, . . .

. . . THEIR COMMANDING OFFICER TRIED ONE DESPERATE PLAN.

THE MEN WERE MUSTERED FOR A ROUT MARCH, AND THEY WERE LOADED WITH WHAT FOOD WAS LEFT AND AS MUCH WATER AS THEY COULD CARRY.

ALL LADDERS AND STAIRS LEADING UP TO THE WALL WERE DESTROYED.

"WE ASSEMBLED ON THE SOUTH WALL AND BEGAN TORMENTING OUR CAPTORS, . . ."

". . . HOPING TO ATTRACT AS MANY AS WE COULD TOWARDS THE MAIN GATE . . ."

". . . WHILE COLONEL DRAX, WITH THE COURAGE OF A MAN POSSESSED, HAD US LOWER HIM ONTO THE PARADE GROUND, WHERE HE, AND HE ALONE, OPENED THE GATE."

"THE COLONEL LED THE ENTIRE MOB WITHIN OUR WALLS."

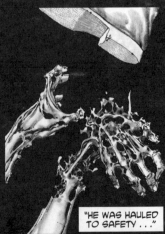

"HE WAS HAULED TO SAFETY . . ."

OFFICIAL FRENCH FOREIGN LEGION RECORDS CONTAIN NO ACCOUNT OF THE SIEGE . . .

. . . NOR DO THEY EXPLAIN WHY A RESCUE PARTY WAS NEVER DISPATCHED TO FORT LOUIS PHILIPPE . . .

. . . OR WHY, ONCE THE SURVIVORS REACHED A NEARBY ARMY GARRISON, THEY WERE ALL BRANDED AS DESERTERS AND IMPRISONED IN FRENCH GUIANA.

NEITHER THE FRENCH NOR THE SUBSEQUENT INDEPENDENT GOVERNMENT OF ALGERIA HAVE EVER SENT AN EXPEDITION TO THE DESERT FORTRESS.

END.

A.D. 1942-45, HARBIN,
JAPANESE PUPPET
STATE OF MANCHUKUO

"OPERATION CHERRY BLOSSOM, . . ."

. . . CONDUCTED BY IMPERIAL JAPAN'S SPECIAL WARFARE UNIT, . . .

. . . INVOLVED EXPERIMENTING ON LIVE HUMAN BEINGS DURING THE SECOND WORLD WAR . . .

. . . TO BREED AN ARMY OF LIVING DEAD.

THEY WERE TO BE USED AGAINST AMERICAN ISLAND BASES, . . .

IF ALL WENT WELL, CHERRY BLOSSOM WOULD ASSURE TOTAL VICTORY FOR IMPERIAL JAPAN.

ALL DID NOT GO WELL.

THE SUBMARINE CARRYING THE UNDEAD STRIKE FORCE NEVER MADE IT TO THE AMERICAN BASE AT ULITHI.

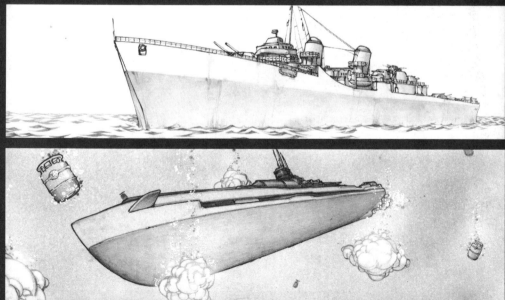

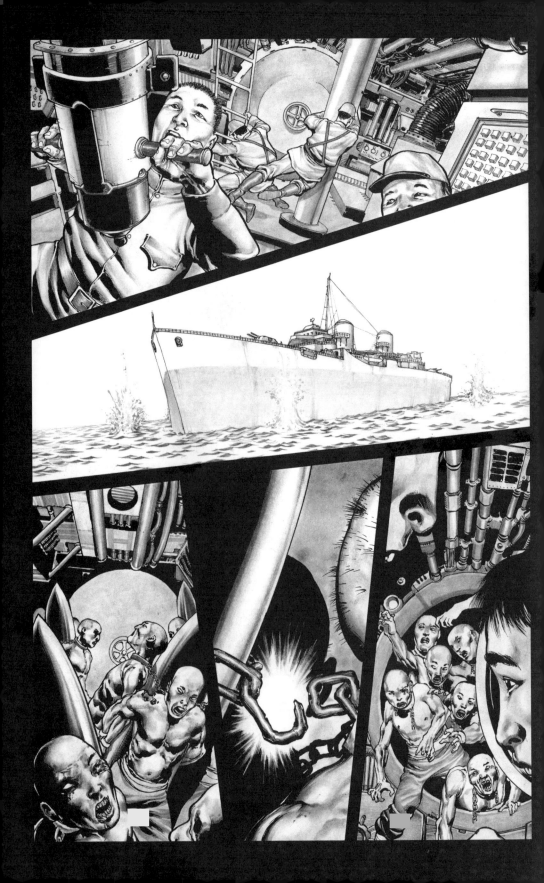

THE ANTI-CHINESE ARMY CAMPAIGN WAS A SIMILAR FAILURE . . .

. . . FOR OBVIOUS REASONS.

THE AIRBORNE ZOMBIES FARED NO BETTER, AS THE "CIVILIAN" ZONE TARGETED FOR INFESTATION WAS ALREADY INFESTED . . .

A.D. 1960, BYELGORANSK,
SOVIET UNION

FIFTEEN YEARS EARLIER, . . .

. . . IT HAD BEEN SUSPECTED . . .

. . . THAT WHEN THE SOVIET UNION INVADED MANCHUKUO . . .

. . . AT THE END OF THE SECOND WORLD WAR, . . .

. . . CERTAIN DOCUMENTS . . .

. . . REGARDING OPERATION CHERRY BLOSSOM . . .

. . . WERE RECOVERED IN SECRET . . .

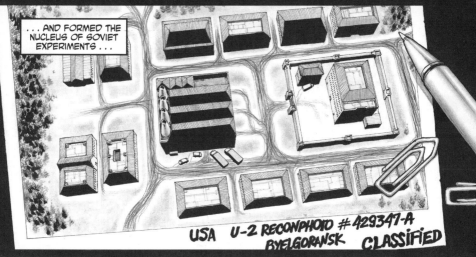

USA U-2 RECONPHOTO #429347-A
BYELGORANSK CLASSIFIED

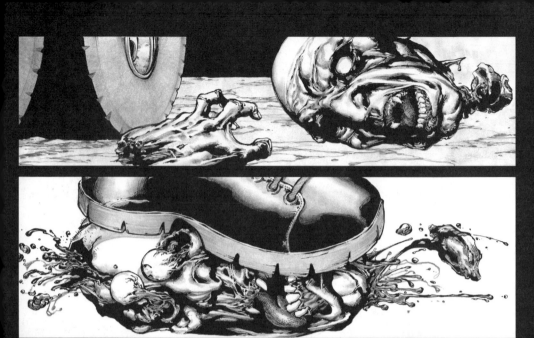

SAFE BEHIND THE PRISON WALLS, . . .

. . . THE TRAPPED COLLECTION OF SOLDIERS AND PRISONERS SETTLED DOWN TO WAIT UNTIL RESCUED.

WELLS WERE DUG, . . .

. . . GREENHOUSES CONSTRUCTED, . . .

. . . AND CONSTANT REPORTS ON THE "SITUATION" . . .

THREE DAYS BEFORE THE AUTUMN FROST, . . .

. . . THE RADIO OPERATOR AT BYELGORANSK REPORTED SPOTTING A LONE AIRCRAFT.

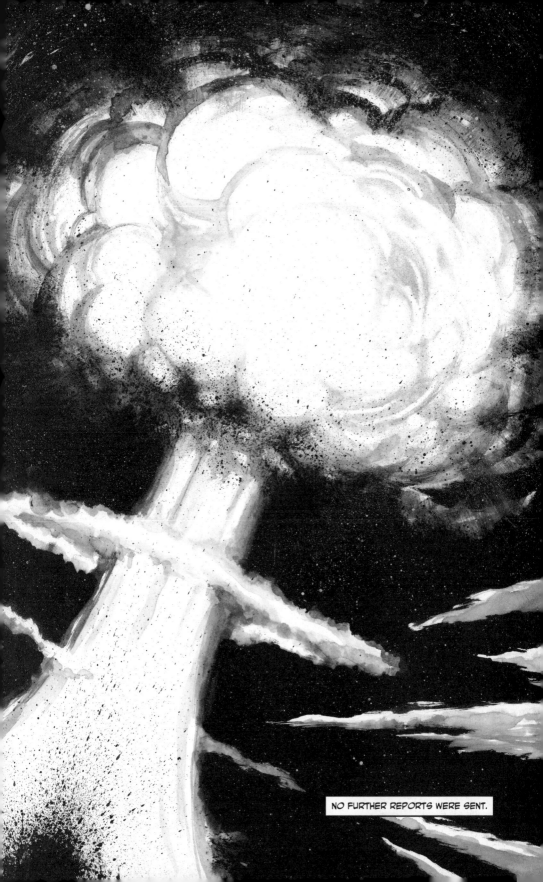

NO FURTHER REPORTS WERE SENT.

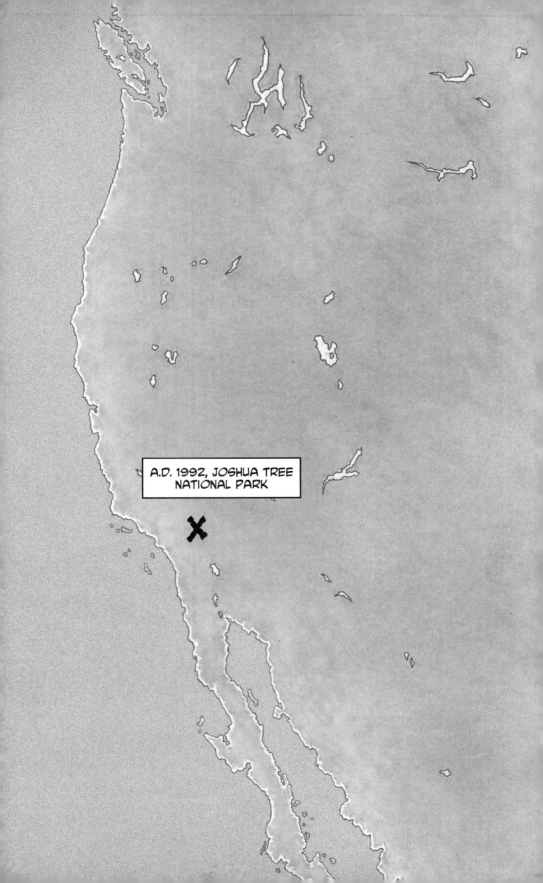

SEVERAL HIKERS AND DAY-TRIPPERS TO THIS DESERT PARK REPORTED AN ABANDONED TENT AND GEAR JUST OFF THE MAIN ROAD.

A FURTHER INVESTIGATION REVEALED HER TO BE SHARON PARSONS OF OXNARD, CALIFORNIA.

SHE AND HER BOYFRIEND, PATRICK MACDONALD, HAD BEEN CAMPING AT JOSHUA TREE FOR SEVERAL DAYS.

ALTHOUGH MACDONALD'S BODY WAS NEVER FOUND, . . .

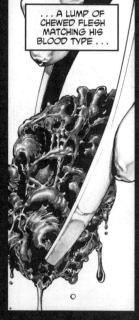

. . . A LUMP OF CHEWED FLESH MATCHING HIS BLOOD TYPE . . .

. . . WAS FOUND LODGED IN SHARON'S ESOPHAGUS.

HOWEVER, TRACES OF SKIN AND FLESH FROM UNDER HER FINGERNAILS MATCH A THIRD PARTY, . . .

DEVIN MARTIN, . . .

. . . A LONER AND WILDLIFE PHOTOGRAPHER, . . .

. . . WHOSE DISAPPEARANCE IN THE PARK WENT UNREPORTED FOR SEVERAL WEEKS.

ONE CAN ONLY SPECULATE . . .

. . . AS TO THEIR MEETING . . .

... AND THE SUBSEQUENT CHAIN OF EVENTS.

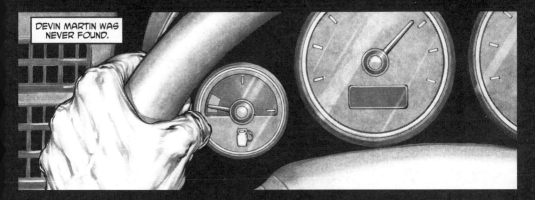

DEVIN MARTIN WAS NEVER FOUND.

NEITHER WAS PATRICK MACDONALD.

HOWEVER, A VIDEO SECURITY CAMERA CAPTURED WHAT LOOKED LIKED MACDONALD AT A GAS STATION IN DIAMOND BAR.

MACDONALD'S CAR WAS LAST SEEN HEADING WEST, ...

... TOWARD LOS ANGELES.

ABOUT THE
AUTHOR

The *New York Times* bestselling author of **THE ZOMBIE SURVIVAL GUIDE** and **WORLD WAR Z, MAX BROOKS** has been called "the Studs Terkel of zombie journalism."

THE END WAS NEAR...

WORLD WAR Z
An Oral History of
the Zombie War
978 0 7156 3703 6
£8.99 paperback

THE WORLDWIDE BESTSELLER

The Zombie War came unthinkably close to eradicating humanity. It began with rumours from China about another pandemic. Then the cases started to multiply and what had looked like the stirrings of a criminal underclass, even the beginnings of a revolution, soon revealed itself to be much, much worse. Suddenly mankind was faced with a future of mindless, cannibalistic horror. Max Brooks, driven by the urgency of preserving the acid-etched firsthand experiences of the survivors from those apocalyptic years, travelled the world recording the testimony of men, women, and sometimes children who came face-to-face with the living, or at least the undead, hell of that dreadful time. *World War Z* is the terrifying result.

'An absolute must have... Brooks infuses his writing with such
precise detail and authenticity, one wonders
if he knows something we don't'
Simon Pegg

'When the zombie apocalypse arrives, we'll be at Max Brooks's
house... as a horror story, it's exciting. As a parable, it's terrifying'
Empire *****

'A cracking read... Brooks has hit gruesome gold with this beauty...
one of the best books I've read all year'
Darkside Magazine

DUCKWORTH OVERLOOK   90-93 COWCROSS STREET   LONDON EC1M 6BF
www.ducknet.co.uk

**THE ZOMBIE
SURVIVAL GUIDE**
Complete Protection
from the Living Dead
978 0 7156 3318 2
£8.99 paperback

WILL YOU SURVIVE THE ZOMBIE WAR?

THE BESTSELLING ZOMBIE SENSATION

Don't be carefree and foolish with your most precious asset: life. *The Zombie Survival Guide* is your key to survival against the hordes of undead who may be stalking you *right now*. Fully illustrated and exhaustively comprehensive, this book covers everything you need to know, including how to understand zombie physiology and behaviour, the most effective defence tactics and weaponry, ways to outfit your home for a long siege, and how to survive and adapt in any territory or terrain. *The Zombie Survival Guide* offers complete protection through trusted, proven tips for safeguarding yourself and your loved ones against the living dead. It is a book that can save your life.

'So meticulous and well researched that it's more scary than funny.
This book lays out everything you need to know to protect yourself
from flesh-eating monsters'
Esquire

'A bloody-minded, straight-laced manual for evading the grasp of the undead'
Time Out

'I doubt that I'll read a more disturbing book this year. Buy it for yourself,
your friends, put a copy next to your toilet. Brilliantly written,
morbidly funny, completely convincing'
Vector

'A tome you start reading for fun and then at page 50 you go out and buy a
machete just to be on the safe side'
New York Post

'Max Brooks is so straightforward, so sensible and logical about everything,
that you start to believe him... This practical approach is exactly what makes
his book *The Zombie Survival Guide* so funny'
Fangoria